I0794802

DK SUPER Planet

Place and Time

MAPPING OUR WORLD

Discover how maps are essential to finding our way around the world

DK

DK Penguin Random House

Produced for DK by
Editorial Just Content Limited
Design Studio Noel

Author Steve Tomecek

Senior Editor Amelia Jones
Senior Art Editor Gilda Pacitti
Managing Editor Katherine Neep
Managing Art Editor Sarah Corcoran
Production Editor Jaypal Chauhan
Production Controller Rebecca Parton
Publisher Sarah Forbes
Managing Director, Learning Hilary Fine

First American Edition, 2025
Published in the United States by DK Publishing,
a division of Penguin Random House LLC
1745 Broadway, 20th Floor, New York, NY 10019

25 26 27 28 29 10 9 8 7 6 5 4 3 2 1
001–345412–Mar/2025

Published in Great Britain by Dorling Kindersley Limited

A catalog record for this book
is available from the Library of Congress.
HC ISBN: 978-0-5939-6262-6
PB ISBN: 978-0-5939-6261-9

Printed and bound in China

www.dk.com

Contents

What Are **MAPS?**

For thousands of years, **maps** have been helping people find their way. A map is a model that shows where things are located in relation to each other. Most maps are flat drawings. This makes it difficult to show round or bumpy things, like Earth. But mapmakers have figured out a way.

Treasure maps show the location of buried treasure. They use **landmarks** like trees and rivers to help treasure seekers find it.

Physical maps use different colors to show what the land looks like, including mountains, forests, and bodies of water.

Political maps show **boundaries**, like **continents**, countries, and cities. Political maps change when boundaries are redrawn.

Fascinating fact

One of the oldest maps in the world comes from what is now Türkiye. It is over 8,000 years old.

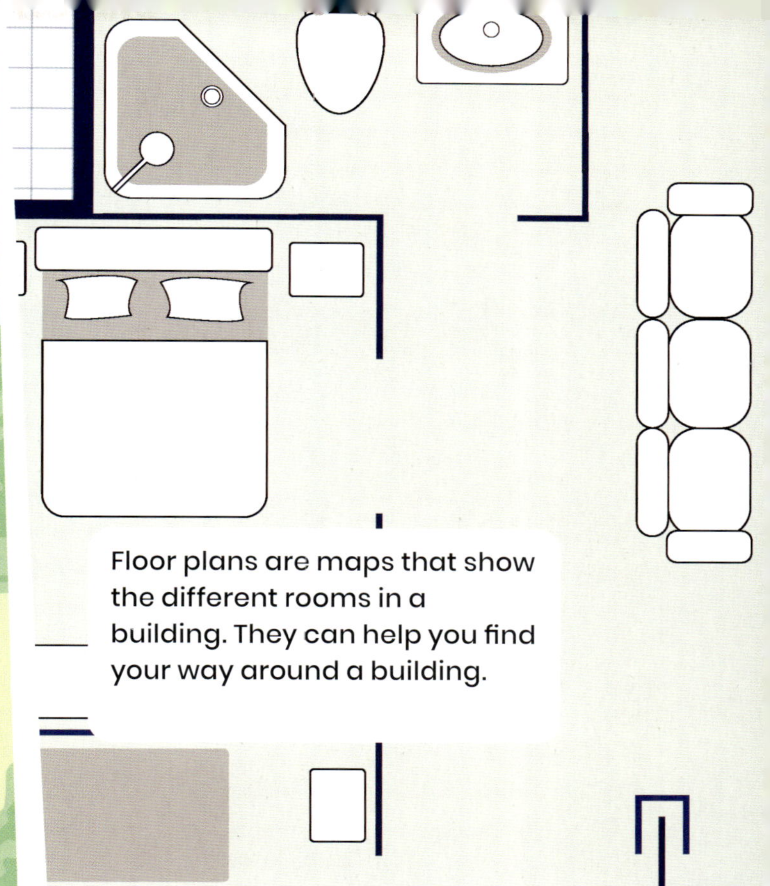

Floor plans are maps that show the different rooms in a building. They can help you find your way around a building.

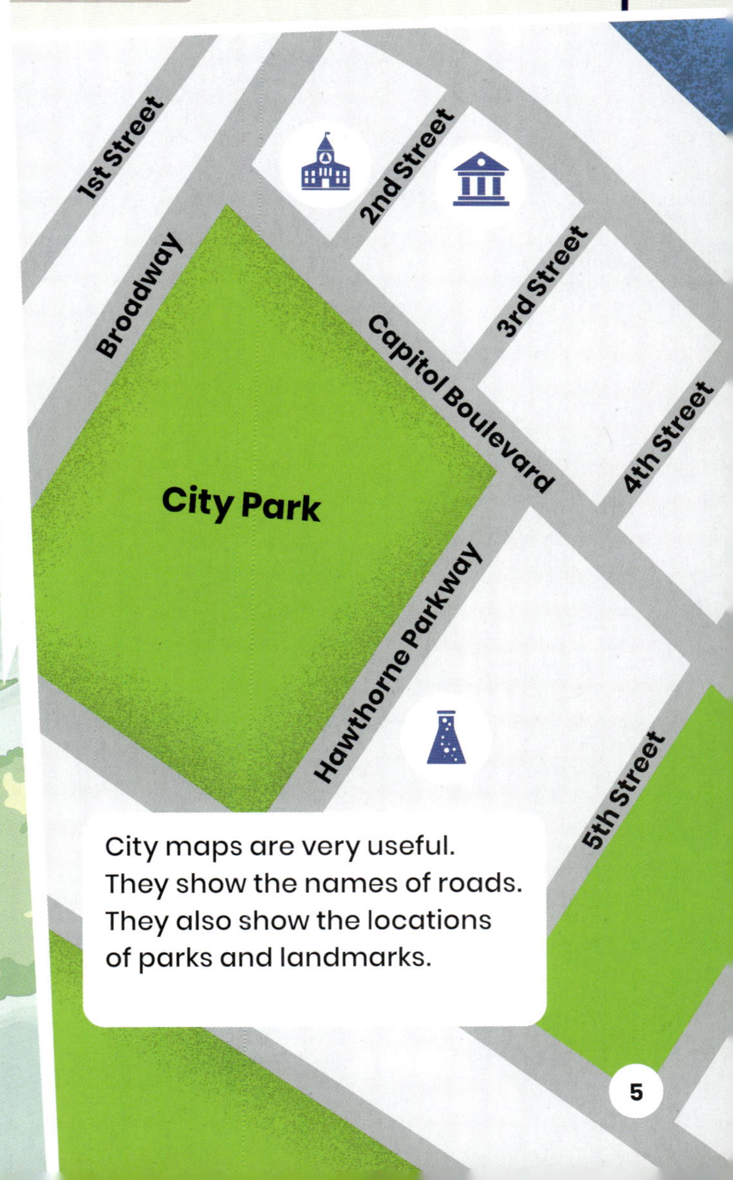

City maps are very useful. They show the names of roads. They also show the locations of parks and landmarks.

Why Do We Need **MAPS?**

Geography is the study of land, people, and the environment around us. One of the most important tools geographers use is maps. Geographers are scientists who use maps to understand the world and its natural features. They also use maps to compare things like **climate**, **population**, and natural resources in different places around the world.

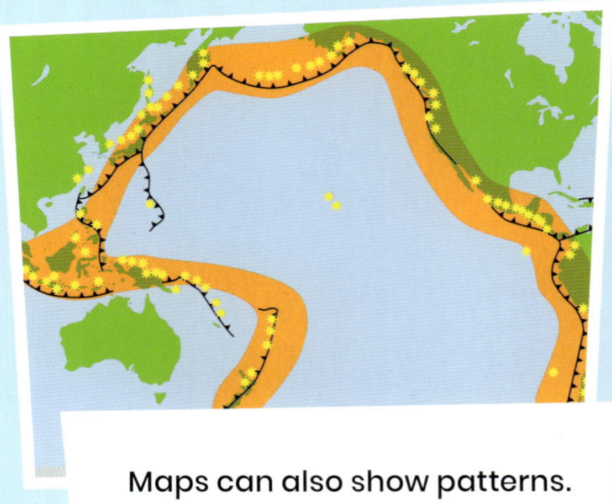

Maps can also show patterns. This map of the Ring of Fire shows earthquake activity in the Pacific Ocean.

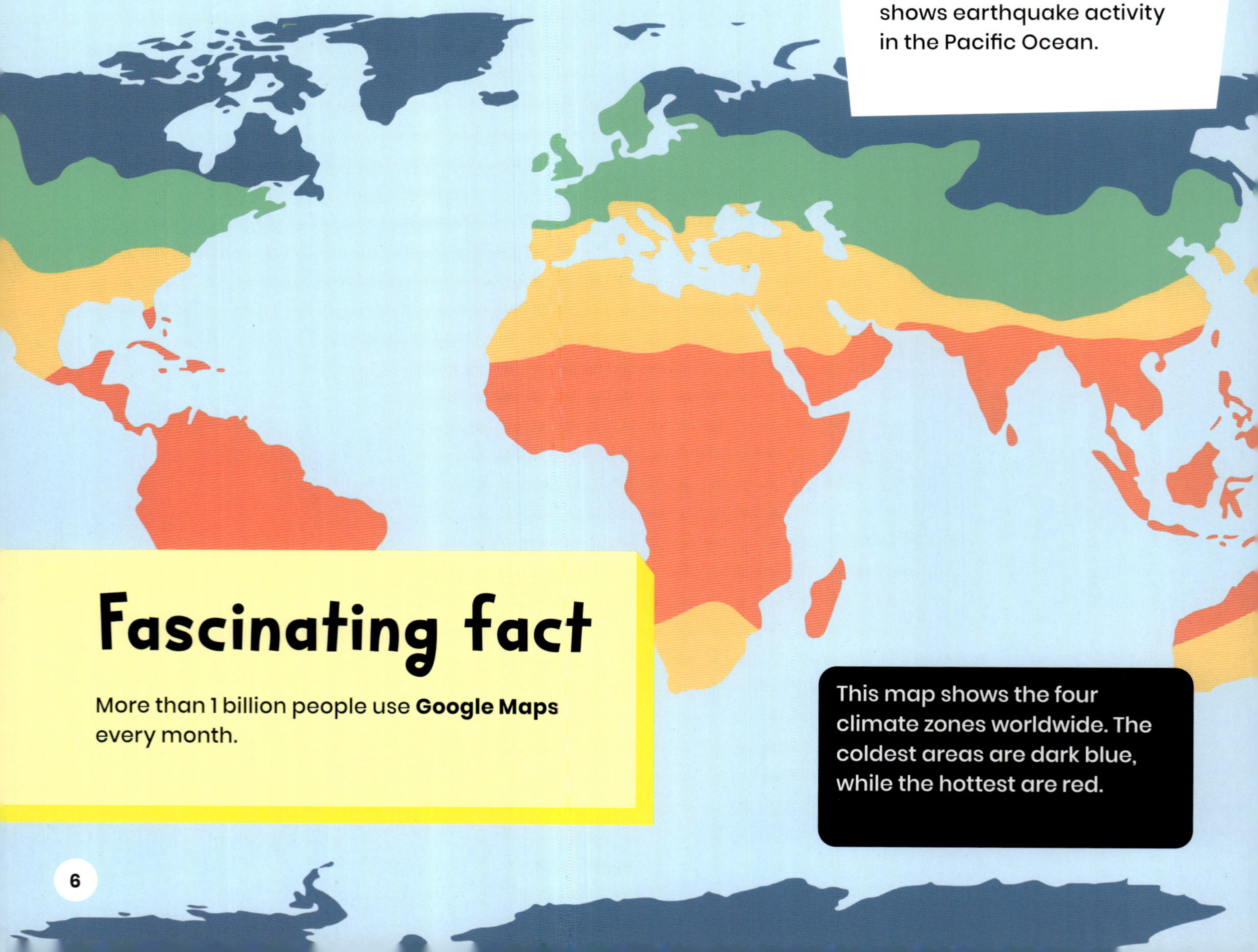

Fascinating fact

More than 1 billion people use **Google Maps** every month.

This map shows the four climate zones worldwide. The coldest areas are dark blue, while the hottest are red.

Maps help people find their way around without getting lost. This is important if you are traveling somewhere new.

Maps can show the **waterways** in a place, like this map of rivers in the USA.

Road maps show how to get from one place to another. They show main roads, smaller roads, and sometimes rest areas.

Trail maps can help you find your way when you are on a hike. They show paths, lakes, streams, hills, and swamps.

Street maps often include locations of famous buildings and other attractions. Some even show bus and train routes.

Map Keys and **SYMBOLS**

People who make maps are called **cartographers**. They use special drawings called map **symbols** to make maps easier to read. These symbols show important features and landmarks. Some show natural features such as rivers, lakes, and mountains. Others show special buildings, such as hospitals, schools, and libraries.

In the past, cartographers drew maps and symbols by hand, like the one shown in the picture above. It is over 400 years old.

Fascinating fact

Map symbols can be traced back over 25,000 years. People who lived in what is now Czechia carved them on a map on a mammoth tusk.

Today, most cartographers use computers to create maps and **keys**. It makes the process quicker and more accurate.

Maps with symbols have a special box called a key or **legend** that tells you what each symbol means.

Map **scale**

0 1 2 km

1 cm

MAP KEY

- City park
- Central bank
- City hospital
- City hall
- River
- Science museum
- City library
- City high school

Map SCALES

Cartographers usually draw maps to scale. This means the **distances** between objects on a map are the same relative size as they are in real life. They are just much smaller. If you want to know the distance between objects on the map, you can use the map scale to calculate it.

On long hikes, people can use map scales to calculate how far they have to travel to get to their next stop.

USING MAP SCALES

Look at the map on the next page. Let's find out the distance between the library and the school.

1. Find the map scale. It looks like a small bar near the map key.

2. The distance marked on the scale tells you that 1 centimeter on this map is equal to 1.24 miles (2 km) in real life.

3. To find the distance between the school and library, use the map scale to measure the distance between the two places in centimeters.

4. Since the scale on this map is 1 cm = 2 km, multiply the distance you measured by 2. This is the actual distance you have to travel between the two places.

Find out!

Use a real map to find out the distance from your house to your school.

Today, cartographers use drones to help them measure distances so that scales are correct.

THE GLOBE

If you want to understand what Earth looks like, you can't beat a **globe**. Think of a globe as a scale model that shows what Earth looks like from space. Globes show the continents and oceans. And most show the world's countries. Geographers have been making and using globes for over 500 years.

Because Earth is shaped like a ball, it is impossible to accurately represent all its features on a flat map.

Fascinating fact

The largest rotating globe in the world is known as Eartha. It is located in Maine. Eartha is over 41.5 ft (12.6 m) in diameter.

Unlike globes, flat maps distort the size of land masses near the poles. Greenland is actually 14 times smaller than Africa.

Some globes show physical features on Earth's surface, such as lakes, rivers, mountain ranges, deserts, and even glaciers.

Maps and globes show many of the same features. But unlike flat maps, globes can accurately show the shapes of the continents.

Most globes have a stand. This allows them to spin and show Earth's tilt as it travels around the Sun.

Compass DIRECTIONS

Before maps, we used the Sun and stars to find our way around. In the **Northern Hemisphere**, the polestar became the direction north. Its opposite became south. Since the Sun rises and sets in a pattern, this gave us the directions east and west. All together, these are the **cardinal directions**.

On a map, a **compass** rose shows the cardinal directions. If you are facing north, then east is on your right.

Compasses can also tell you where north is. Magnetic compasses were first invented more than 2,000 years ago.

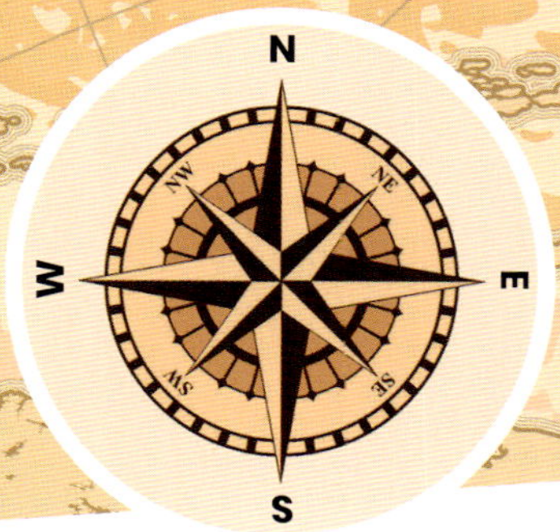

All modern maps have something called a compass rose or a north arrow. This helps you turn the map in the direction you would like to face.

To use a magnetic compass, hold it flat. Slowly turn until the needle points to the letter N. You are now facing north.

Fascinating fact

The word compass comes from Latin. It means "step together."

The needle points to Earth's magnetic pole. This is not the same as true north, which is at the very top of Earth.

Some people still use the Sun and the stars to help them find their way.

Latitude and **LONGITUDE**

If you look at a world map, you will see a pattern of lines crossing each other. This grid is made of lines of **latitude** and **longitude**. These imaginary lines help people describe where different places on Earth are. They also help people locate or **navigate** to different places.

Coordinates are special numbers that help us find the exact location of a place on a map. They are written like this: latitude, longitude.

Since Earth is a sphere, latitude and longitude are measured in degrees. Degrees are also used to measure a circle.

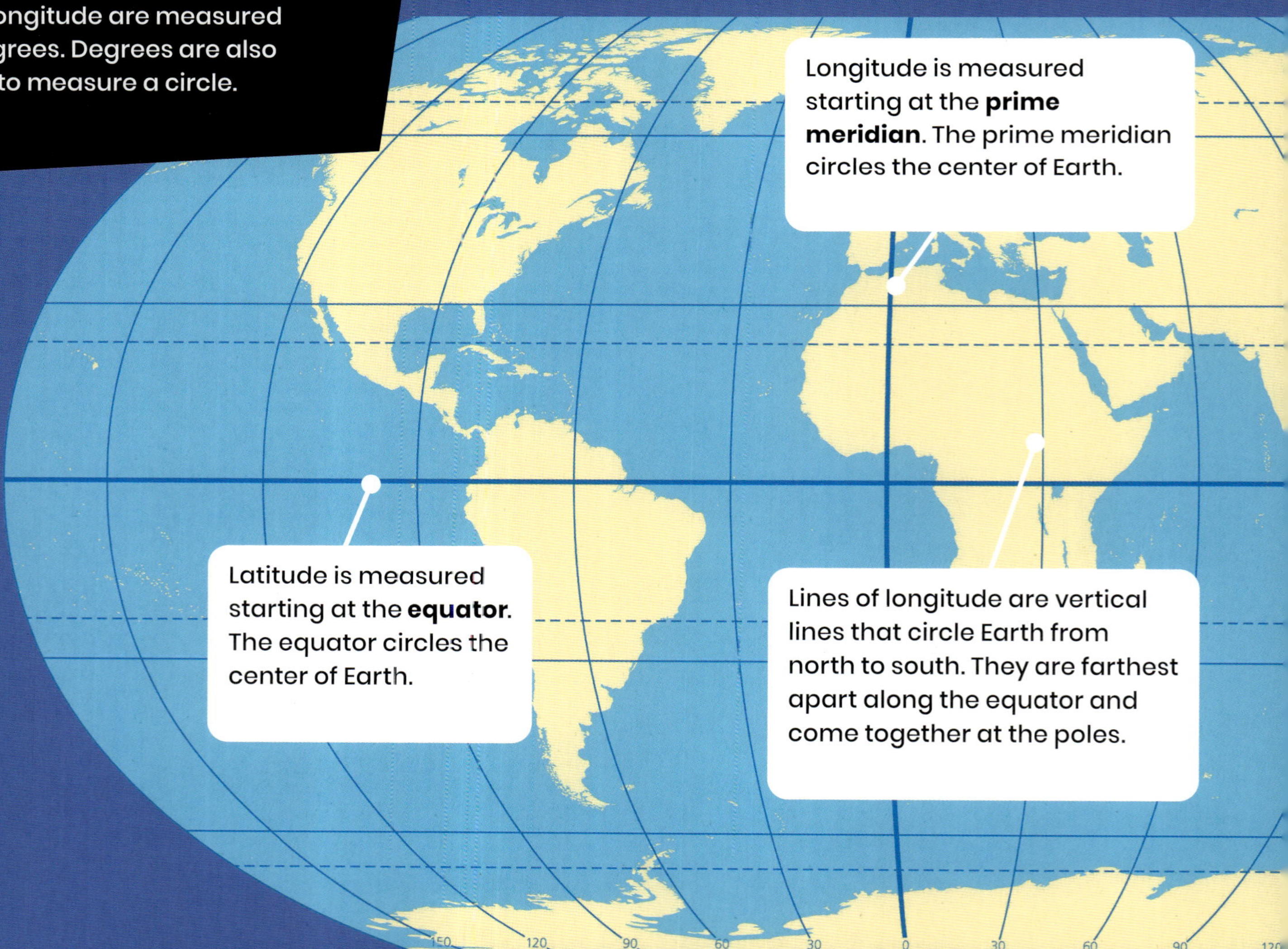

Longitude is measured starting at the **prime meridian**. The prime meridian circles the center of Earth.

Latitude is measured starting at the **equator**. The equator circles the center of Earth.

Lines of longitude are vertical lines that circle Earth from north to south. They are farthest apart along the equator and come together at the poles.

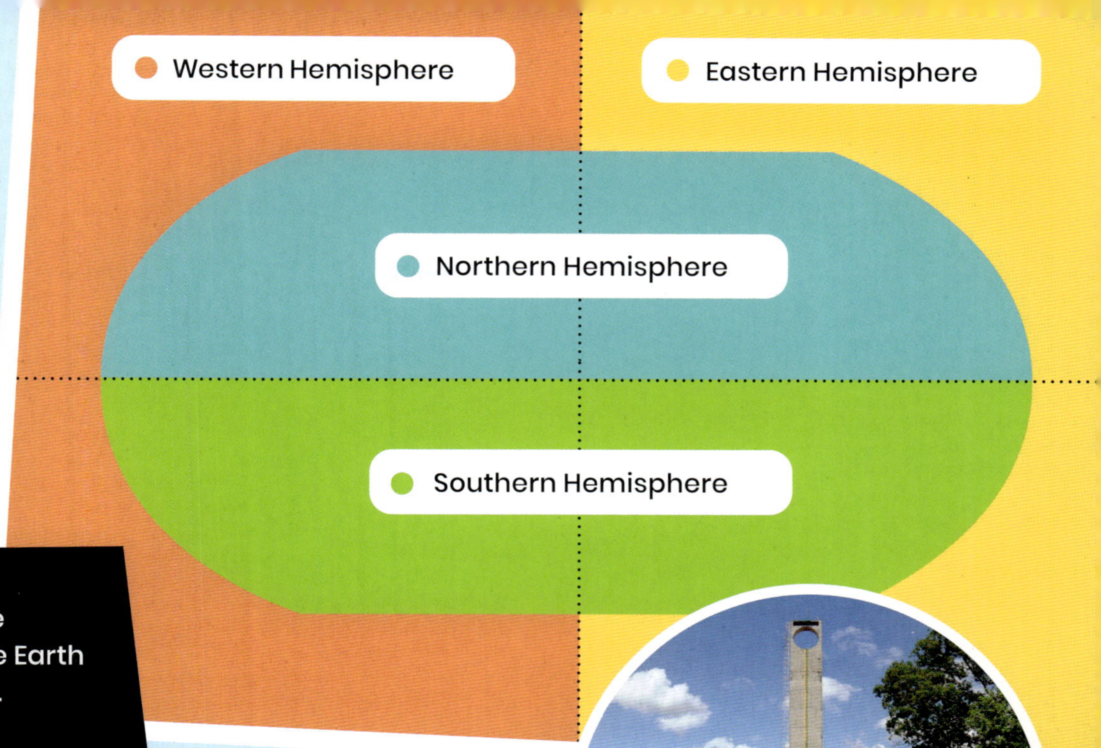

We use lines of latitude and longitude to divide Earth into four **hemispheres**.

Macapá is a city in Brazil that sits right on the Equator. There's a place called the Marco Zero monument where you can stand with one foot in the Northern Hemisphere and the other in the Southern Hemisphere, at the same time. It's like being in two different parts of the Earth all at once!

Lines of latitude are horizontal lines that circle Earth from east to west. They are parallel to each other, which means they never cross.

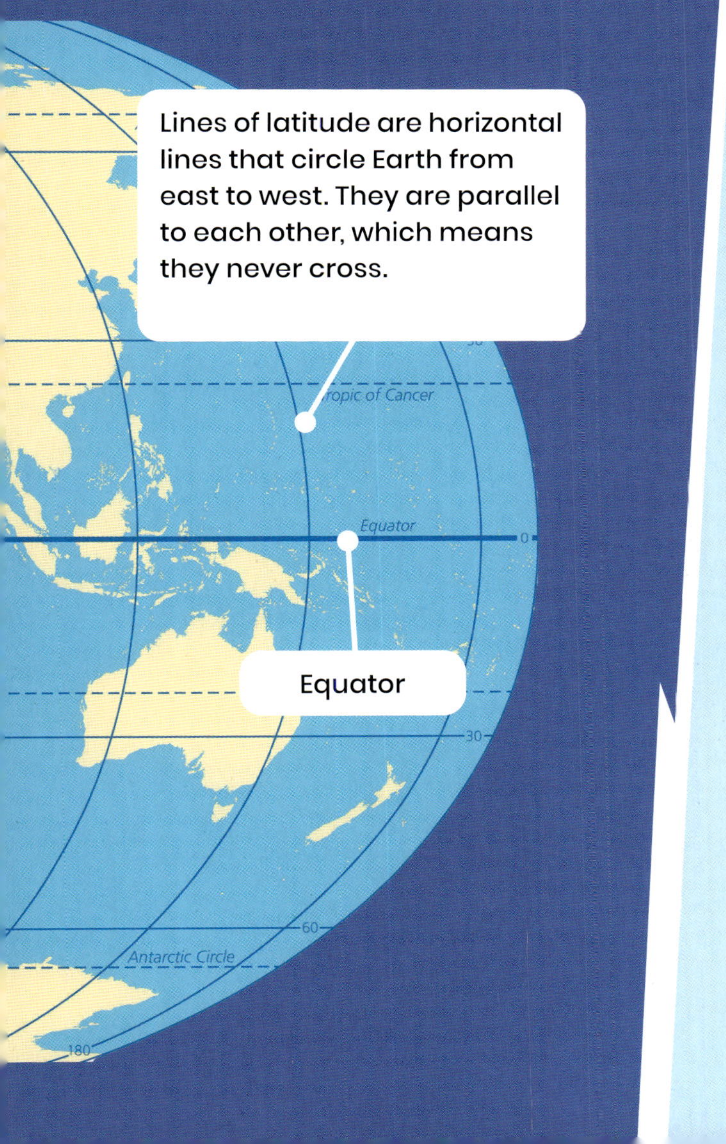

Find out!

What is the latitude and longitude of the place where you live?

Longitude and **TIME ZONES**

Earth is divided into **time zones.** Before the 19th century, these time zones did not exist. But as the world relied more on trains, the need for standardized time zones grew. In 1876, an engineer proposed dividing the world into 24 time zones.

As you move east from the prime meridian, you gain one hour for each time zone. As you move west, you lose one hour.

The prime meridian runs through Greenwich, in London, UK. It is set as the 0 hour.

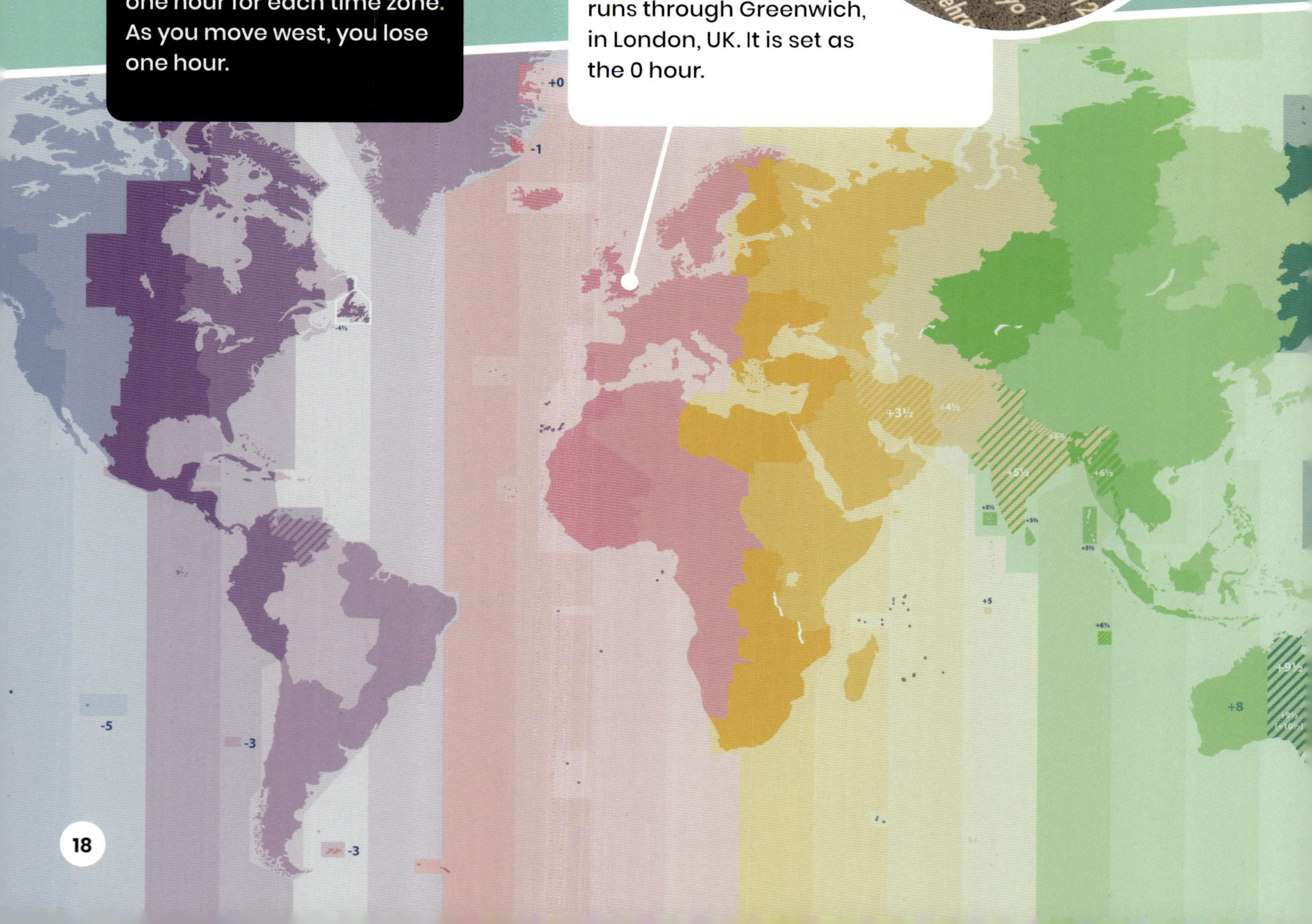

The **international date line** runs opposite the prime meridian.

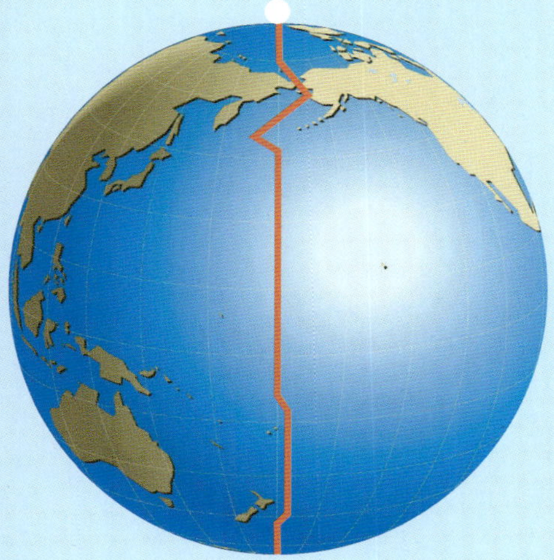

The US has six time zones.

If you keep changing time zones, you will eventually run out of hours in the day. This is why we have the international date line.

When you cross west over the international date line, you jump ahead one day. If you cross east, you turn back one day. Tokyo, Japan, is almost a full day ahead of Honolulu, Hawai'i. If it is 8am on a Monday in Honolulu, that means it is 3am on Tuesday in Tokyo.

Fascinating fact

The international date line bends around several islands in the Pacific Ocean. This is so the islands are not split into two different days.

HEMISPHERES

The equator divides Earth into the Northern and Southern Hemispheres. Most of the land masses on Earth are found in the Northern Hemisphere. These include Europe, Asia, North America, about half of Africa, and a small piece of South America. The rest of South America, plus Australia and Antarctica, are in the Southern Hemisphere.

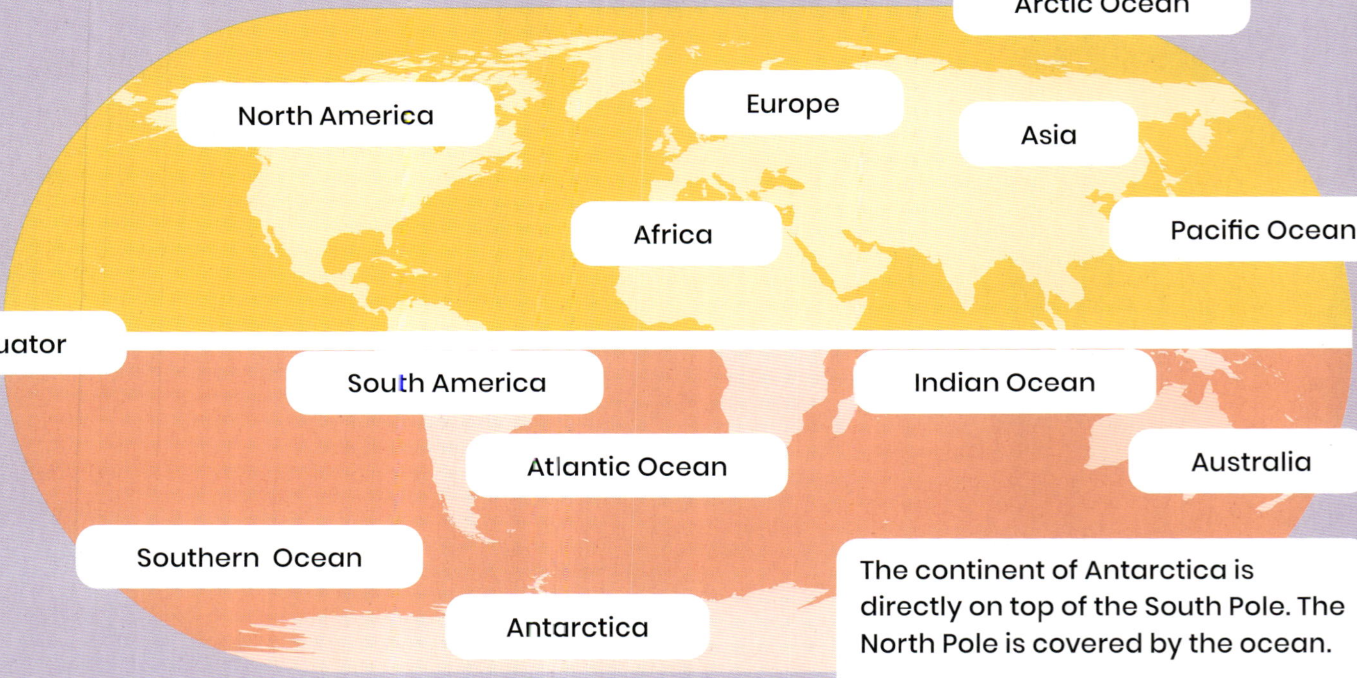

The continent of Antarctica is directly on top of the South Pole. The North Pole is covered by the ocean.

Fascinating fact

If you are in the Northern Hemisphere, the June **solstice** marks the start of summer. But if you are in the Southern Hemisphere, it is the December solstice that starts summer.

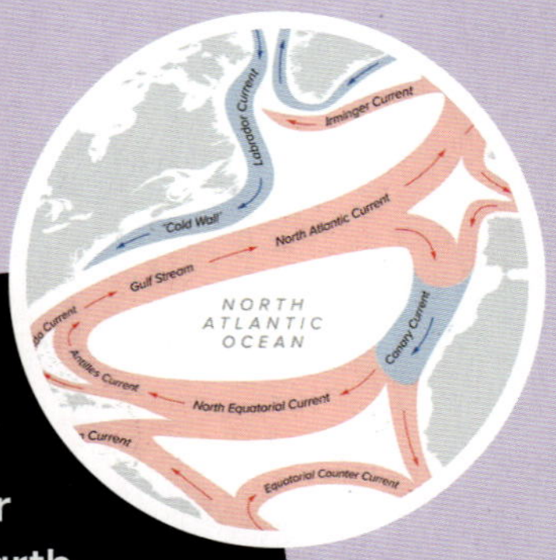

The poles affect how ocean water moves around Earth. This impacts climate and weather patterns on the continents.

It takes about one year for Earth to **orbit** the Sun. Because Earth's axis is tilted, it affects how sunlight hits Earth's surface.

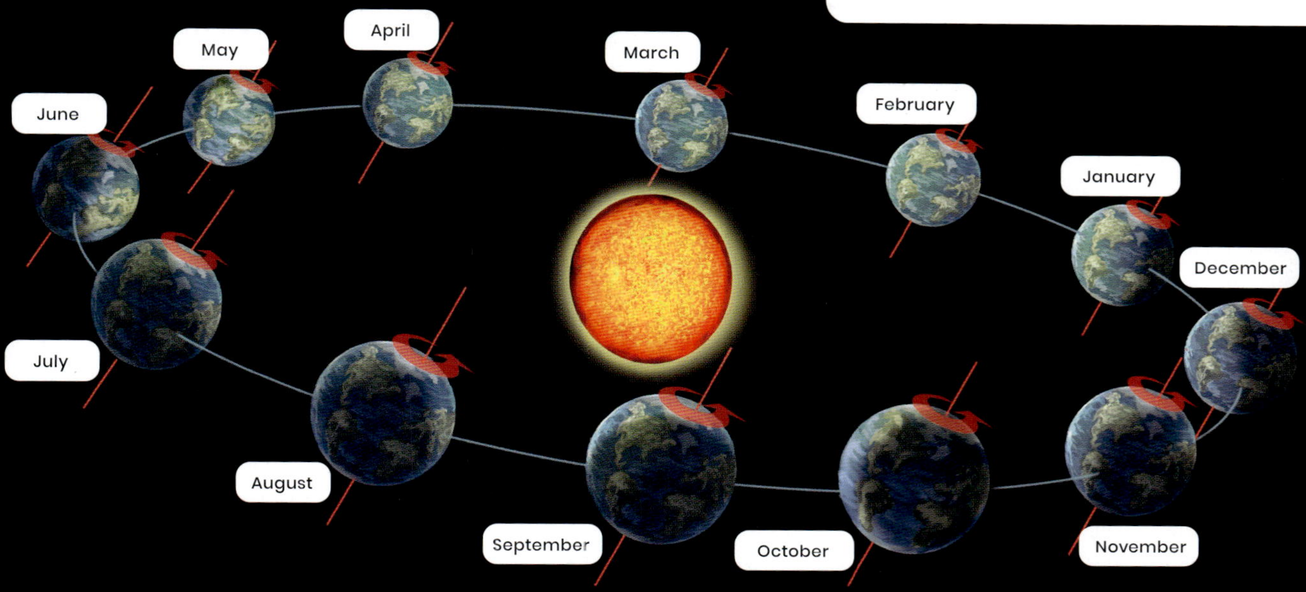

Earth spins around an imaginary line called the **axis** of **rotation**. Earth's rotation is what gives us day and night.

The Northern and Southern Hemispheres get different amounts of sunlight at different times of the year. This gives us **seasons**.

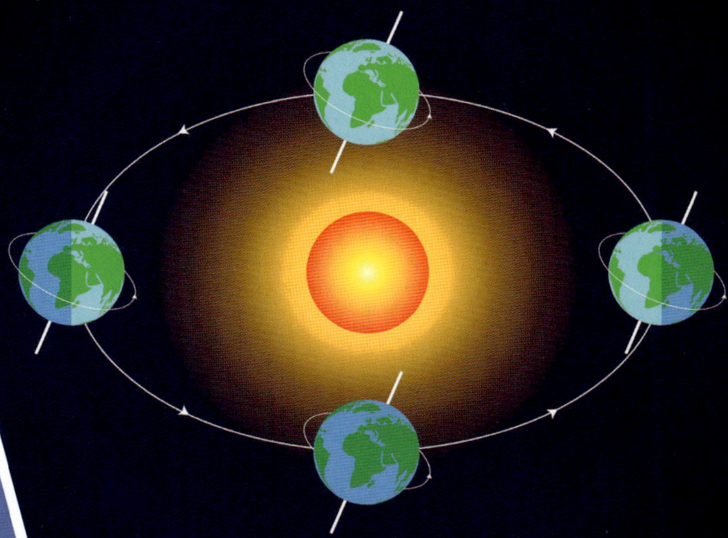

Topographic and **PHYSICAL MAPS**

To get a sense of what Earth's surface looks like, you need to use a physical map. Physical maps show major cities and towns, but their main purpose is to show landforms and bodies of water. Some show the **elevations** of mountains and the locations of other features, like forests and deserts.

Physical maps show information about Earth's surface. On the map below, you can see lakes, rivers, and mountain ranges of North America.

This three-dimensional physical map shows a part of Colorado. It helps show what the surface of the land looks like.

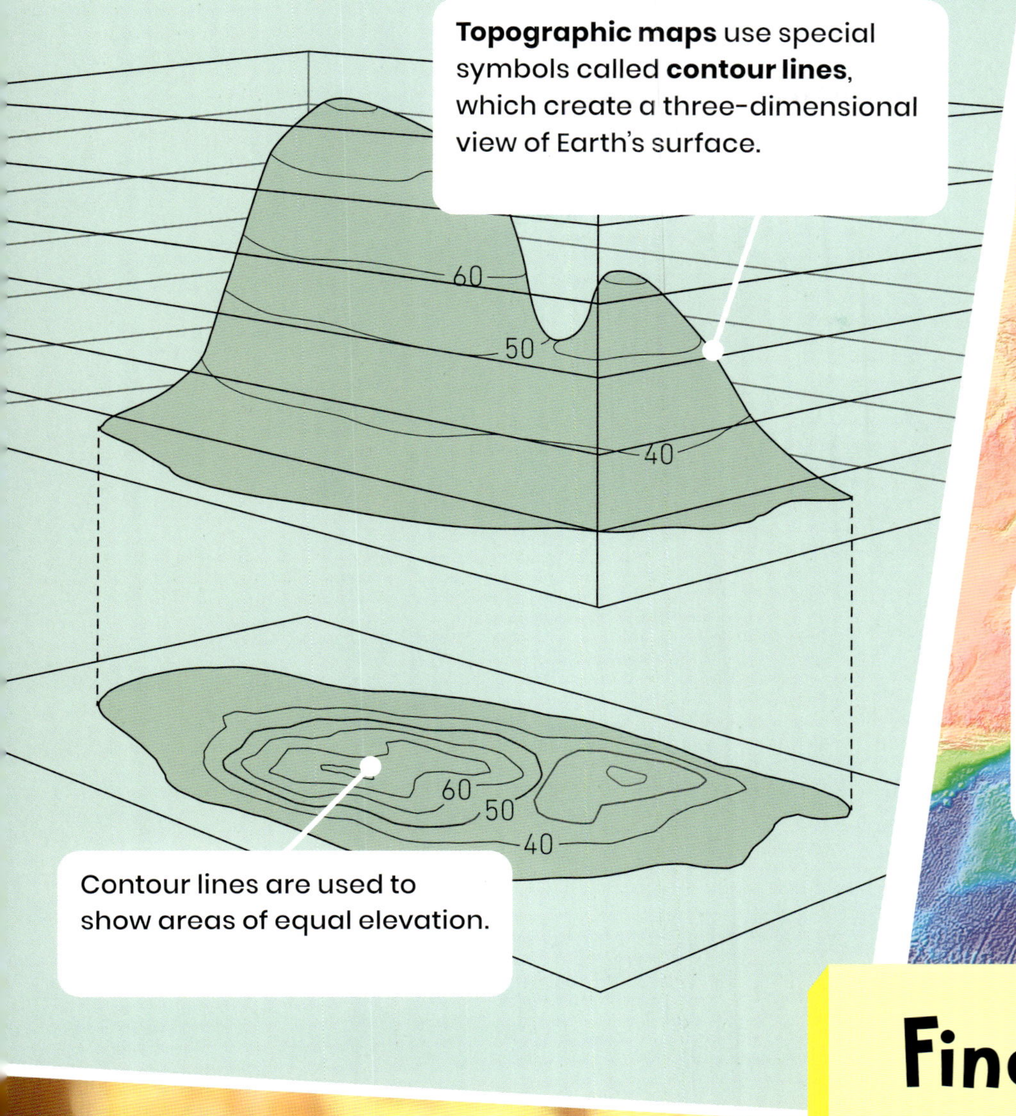

Topographic maps use special symbols called **contour lines**, which create a three-dimensional view of Earth's surface.

Contour lines are used to show areas of equal elevation.

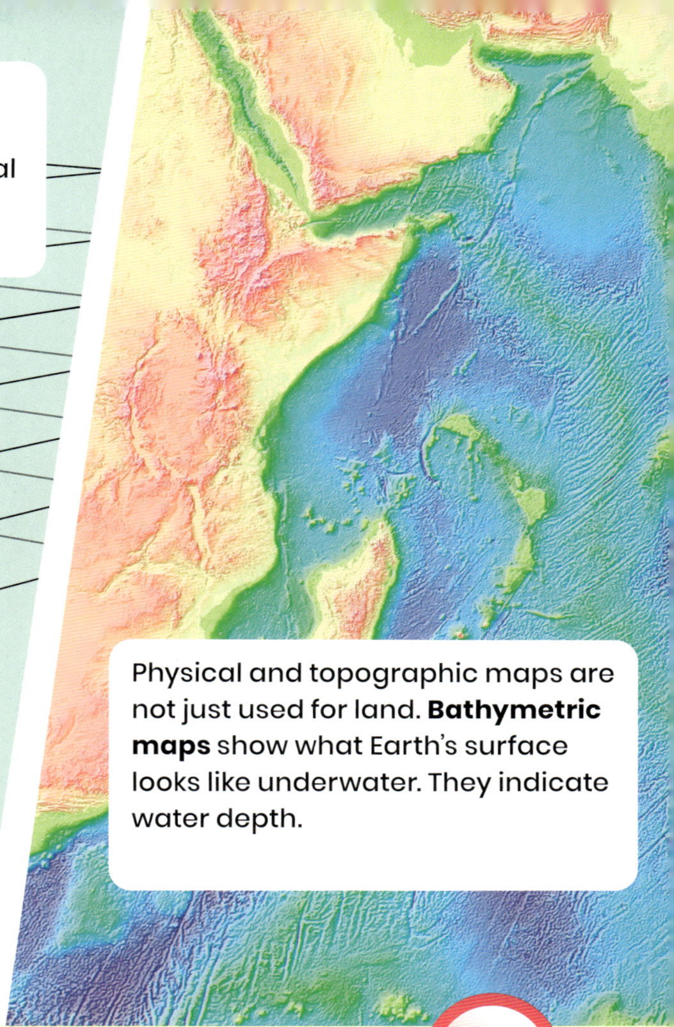

Physical and topographic maps are not just used for land. **Bathymetric maps** show what Earth's surface looks like underwater. They indicate water depth.

Find out!

Can you find a topographic map of your area? Check your local library or ask your teacher.

Hikers, engineers, and scientists use topographic maps to understand what physical features are present in an area.

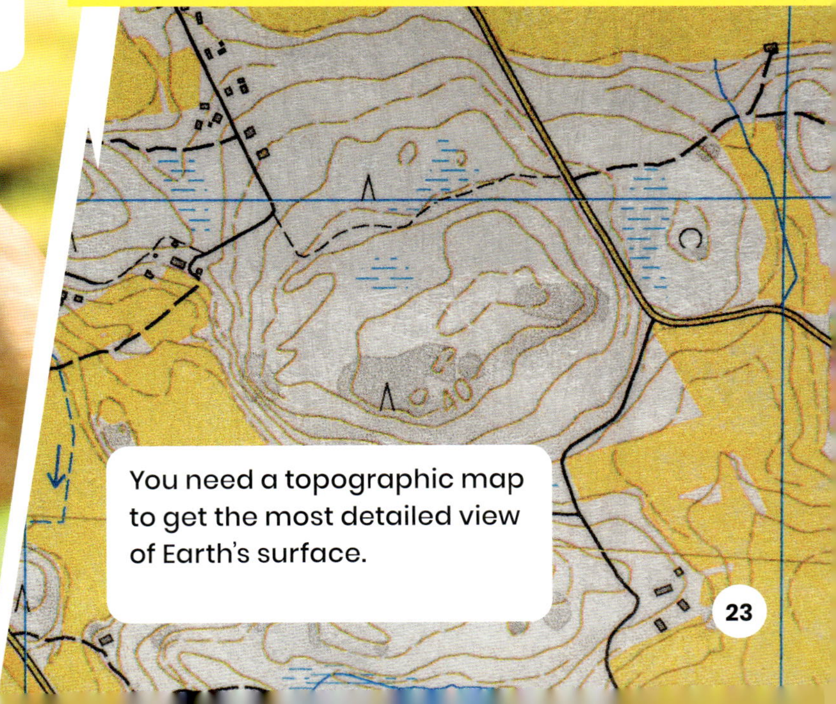

You need a topographic map to get the most detailed view of Earth's surface.

Historical
MAPS

Since people first started making them, maps have changed a lot. One big change is the material they are made with. Today, most maps are printed on paper. But long ago, maps were carved on materials like stones and clay tablets. These historical maps can give us clues about the people who made them.

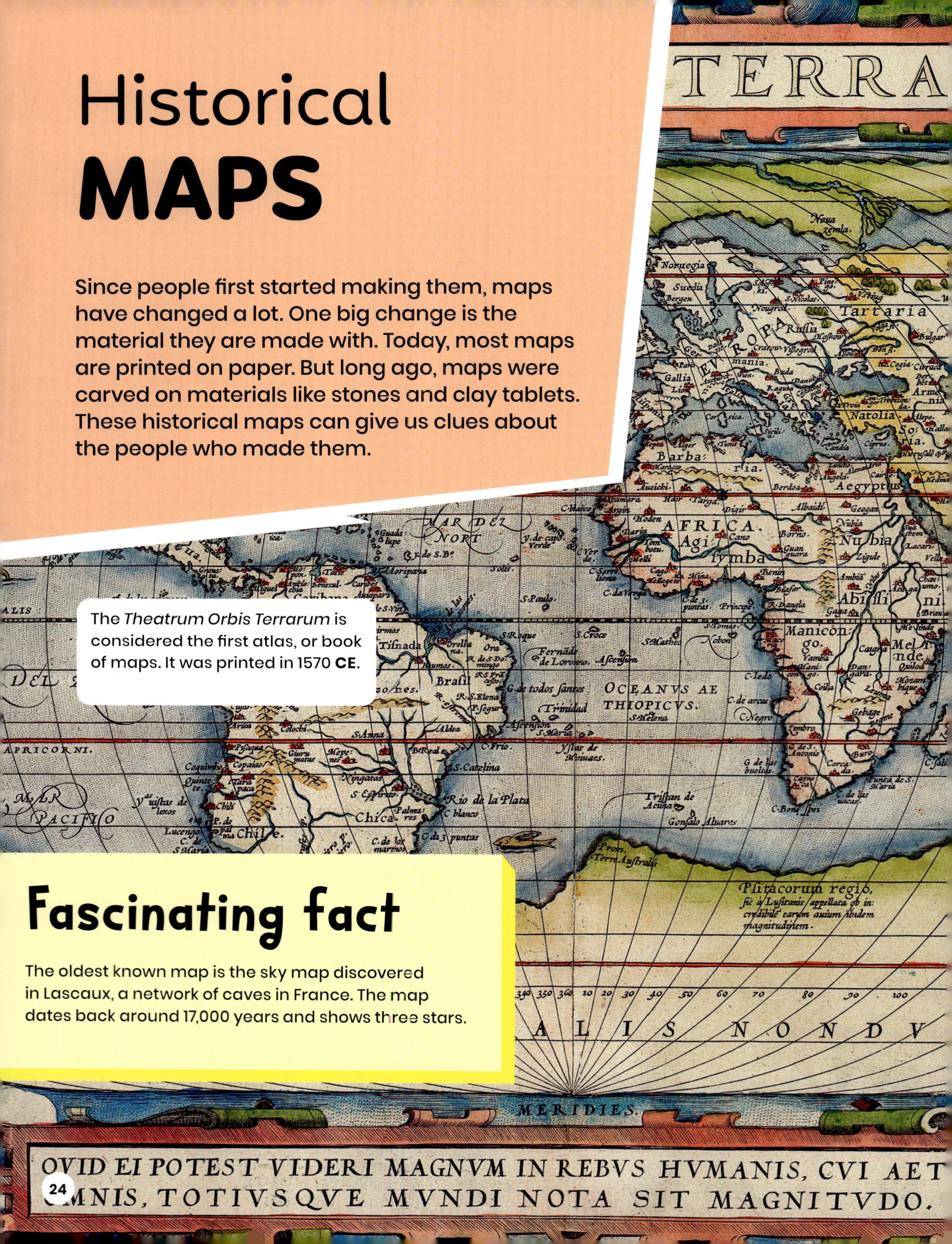

The *Theatrum Orbis Terrarum* is considered the first atlas, or book of maps. It was printed in 1570 **CE**.

Fascinating fact

The oldest known map is the sky map discovered in Lascaux, a network of caves in France. The map dates back around 17,000 years and shows three stars.

The Imago Mundi map was carved into clay around the 6th century **BCE**. It shows Babylon, surrounding areas, and bodies of water.

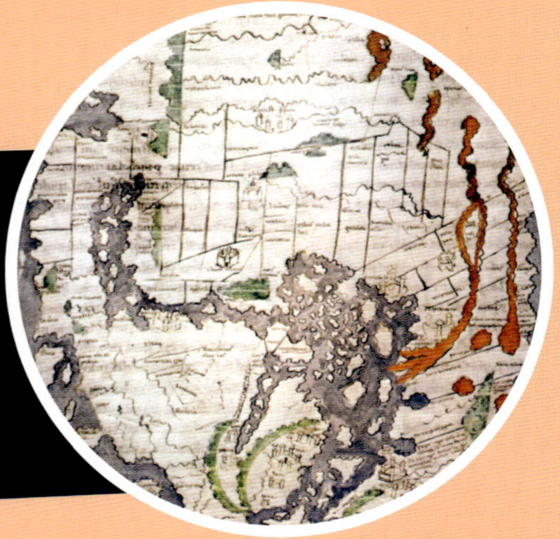

This Anglo-Saxon world map was made between 1025 and 1050 CE. It is probably based on a Roman map.

The Turin Papyrus Map dates to around 1150 BCE. It shows where stone quarries were located in Ancient Egypt.

The Bedolina Map was carved into rock between 1000 and 200 BCE. It is one of the oldest topographic maps, and shows fields and villages.

Thematic **MAPS**

Information about what is happening in different places around the world can be presented in maps. This allows people to compare them and see changes over time. Maps that show specific information are called thematic maps. They can show things that relate to an area's climate, **economy**, or population.

Thematic maps can show lots of information about people, including their age, their education, and how much money they have. They can make complicated information simpler to understand.

Thematic maps are not just about people. They are about places, too. This map shows how much water is available around the world. The lighter blue areas have less water, and the darker blue ares have more.

In order to collect accurate data for thematic maps, measurements need to be taken around the world.

A population density map shows how many people live in an area. They are mostly used by official organizations.

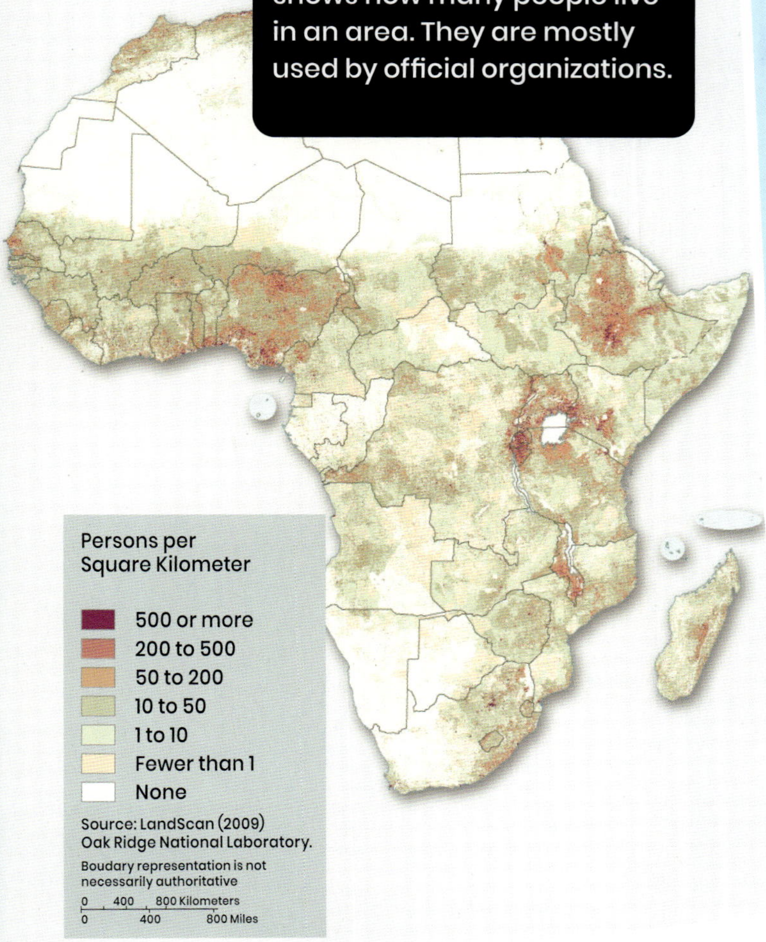

A climate map shows the different climate zones in an area. It uses varied colors to show each zone.

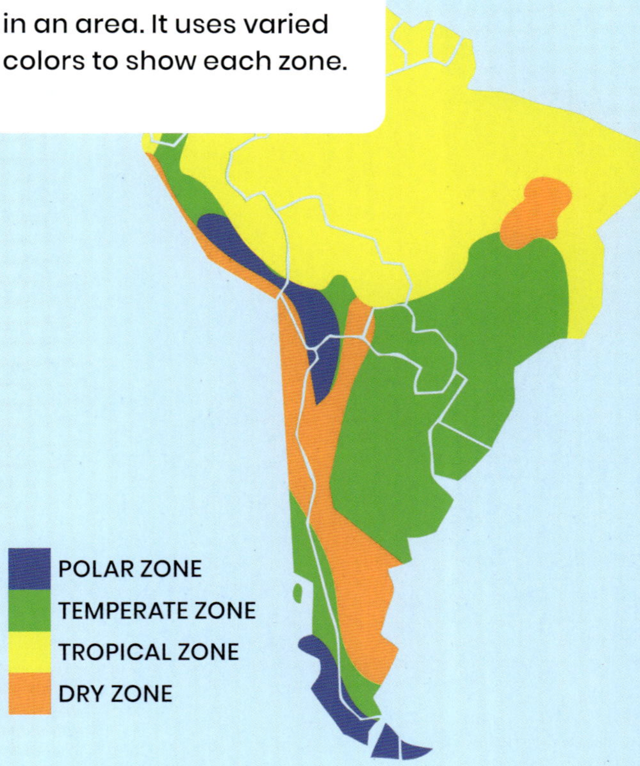

Thematic maps can show useful information to help people understand environments. This map shows deforestation in South-East Asia.

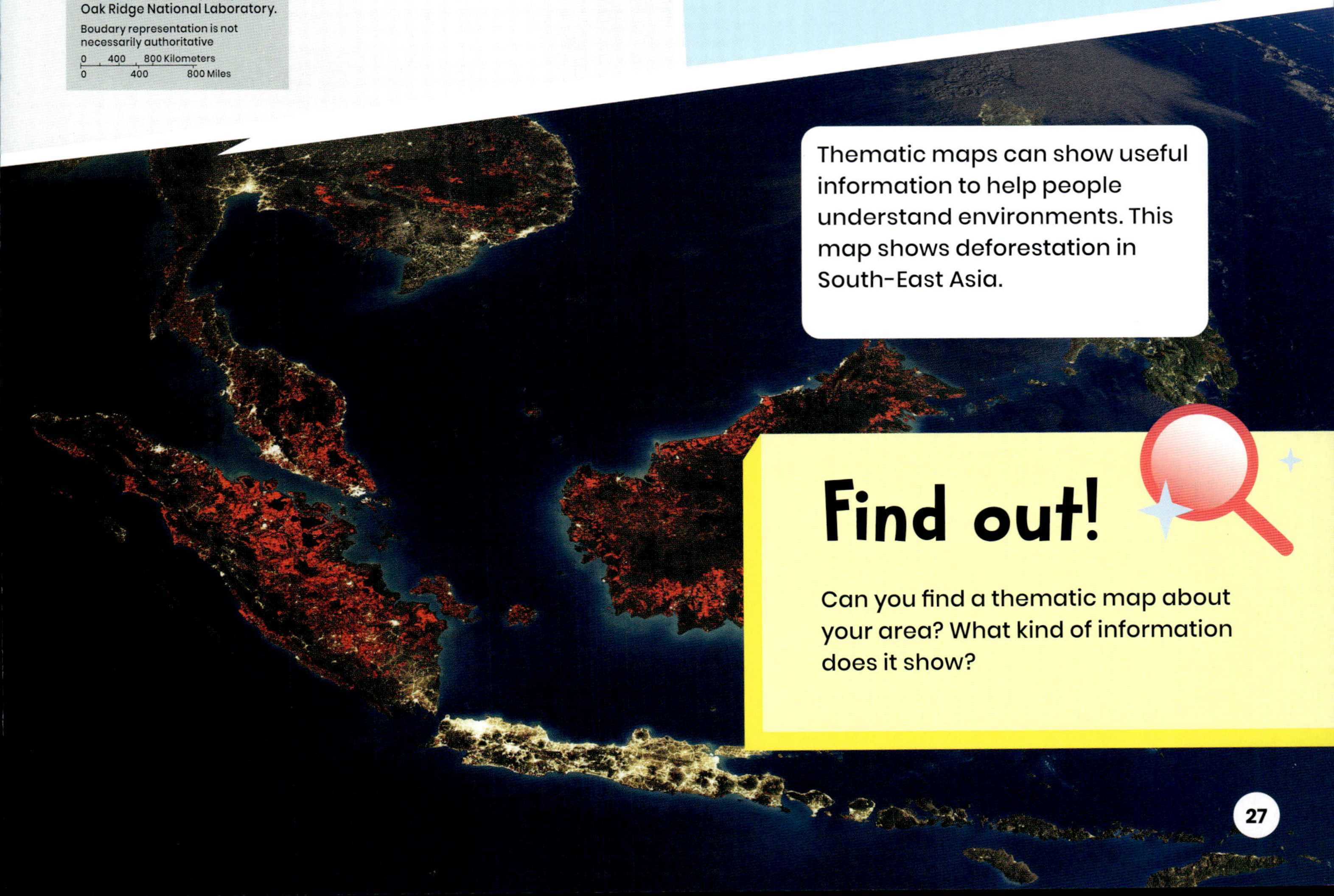

Find out!

Can you find a thematic map about your area? What kind of information does it show?

Mapping
CLIMATE CHANGE

Scientists can use maps to track the impact of climate change. Maps can help scientists monitor climate data, like temperatures. They can also compare conditions in the past to the present. This lets scientists see where problems are and how fast changes are happening.

Scientists use maps to make predictions. They come up with solutions to help reduce climate change's impact in the future.

Scientists use satellites to make detailed maps of Earth. These two maps show that Arctic ice has shrunk dramatically between 1980 and 2012.

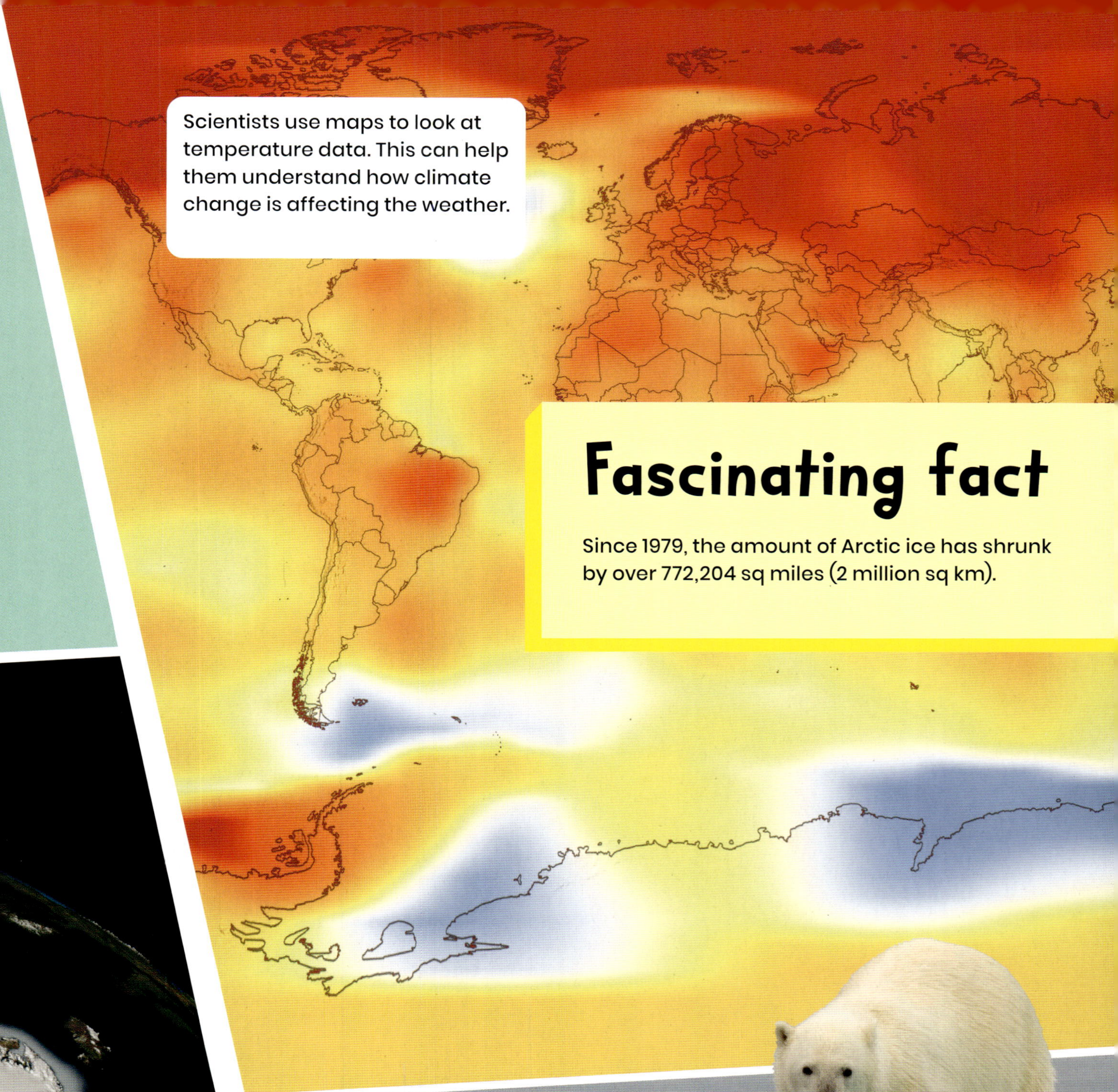

Scientists use maps to look at temperature data. This can help them understand how climate change is affecting the weather.

Fascinating fact

Since 1979, the amount of Arctic ice has shrunk by over 772,204 sq miles (2 million sq km).

Warmer weather melts the ice in the polar regions, affecting the habitats of many animals.

Transit **MAPS**

Imagine you have arrived in a new city. You want to use public transportation to get around. The best way to figure out which bus or train to take is to use a transit map. These maps show different routes in different colors. They include stops and transfer points. Some show major attractions, like museums, schools, libraries, and government buildings.

More than 3 million people ride the New York City subway each day.

Subway maps use something called schematization. It means that the lines on the map are straightened out, and the stations are spaced evenly so that they're easy to find.

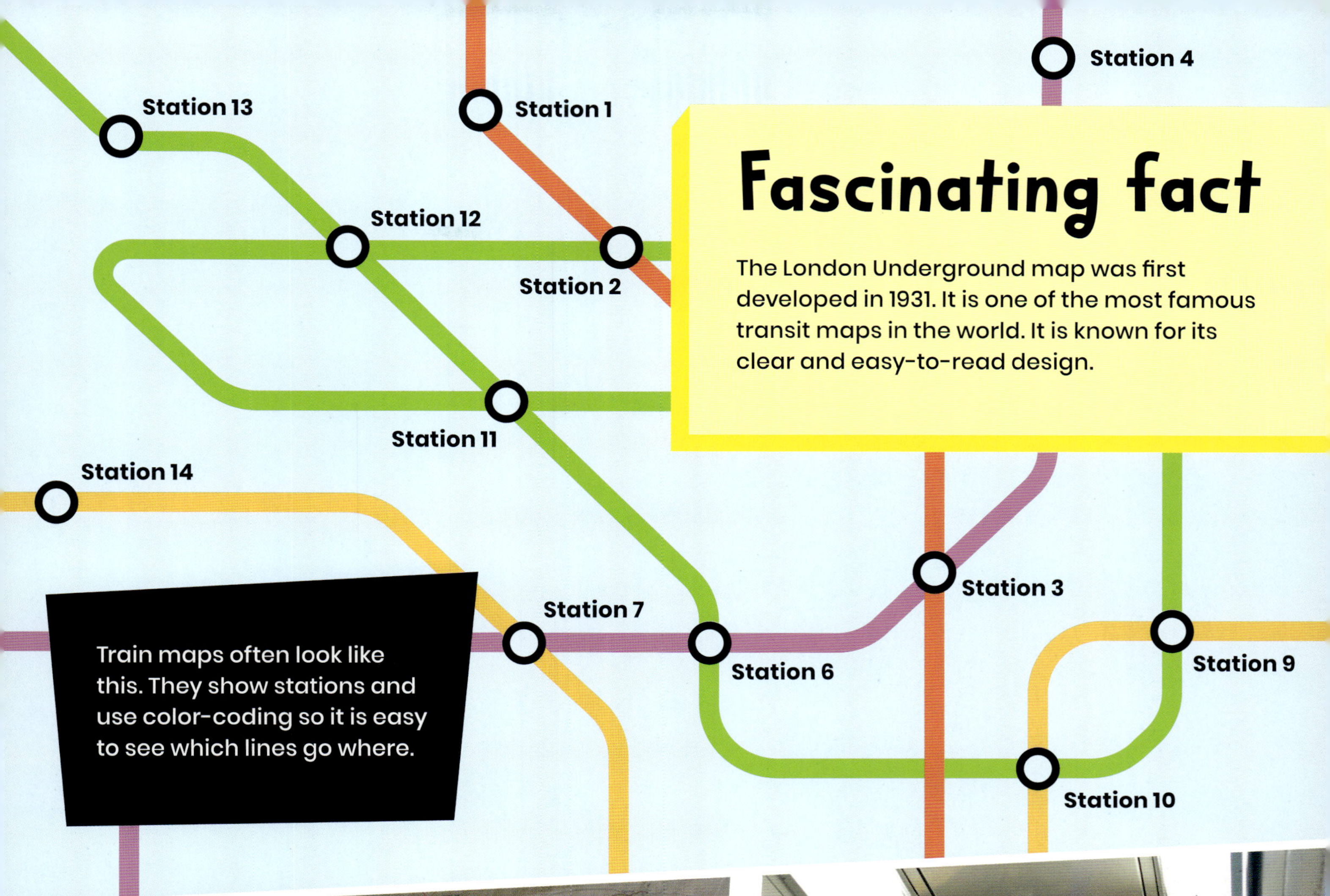

Train maps often look like this. They show stations and use color-coding so it is easy to see which lines go where.

Fascinating fact

The London Underground map was first developed in 1931. It is one of the most famous transit maps in the world. It is known for its clear and easy-to-read design.

Bus maps often show timetables, ticket prices, and routes.

The London Underground travels a total length of around 250 miles (402 km) across its network.

Modern **MAPPING**

For centuries, maps have been printed on paper. Now more people are using digital maps. Digital maps have many advantages over printed maps. They can be updated almost instantly. And they can put the world in the palm of your hand. They are also scalable. You can zoom out to a country or zoom in to street level.

Thanks to the Global Positioning System (GPS), your phone can show your exact location when you open a map app.

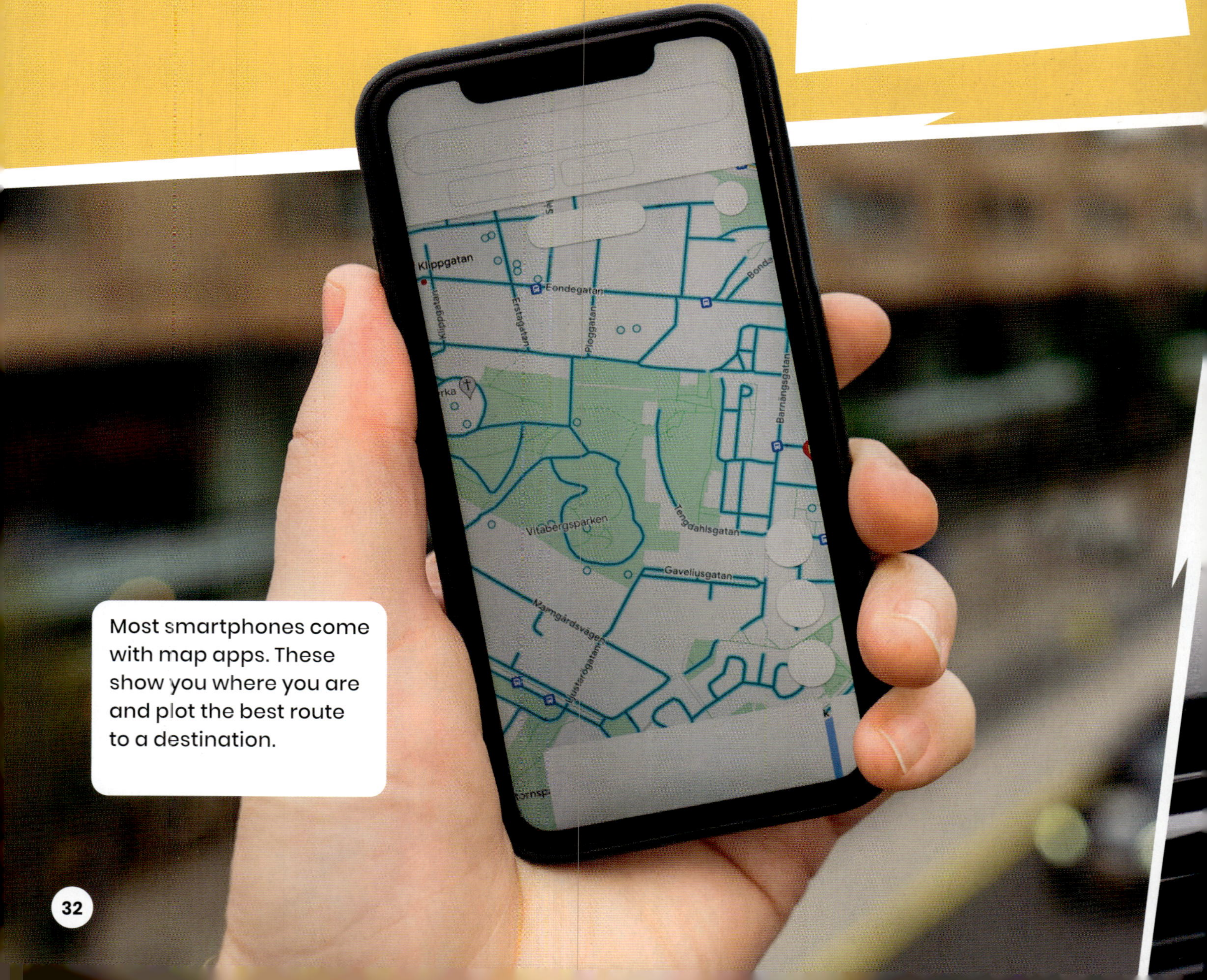

Most smartphones come with map apps. These show you where you are and plot the best route to a destination.

GPS provides data for digital maps. GPS works using data from satellites.

Fascinating fact

GPS satellites orbit Earth at a distance of about 12,550 miles (20,200 km) and complete two orbits each day.

Satellite navigation systems (satnav) also use GPS. Most modern cars come with satnav.

Everyday **SCIENCE**

Navigating by the Stars

Before we had compasses and GPS, we navigated using the stars. If you live in the Northern Hemisphere, you can use **Polaris**, or the North Star, to get around at night. Polaris is not as bright as you might think. As Earth rotates, other stars seem to move. But Polaris stays in the same place.

Polaris is directly over the North Pole, which is why it does not appear to move at night.

Sailors use a piece of equipment called a sextant to see the angle of Polaris in the sky. It tells them how far north they are.

Polaris
Since Polaris is over the North Pole, it always points north. Once you find it, you can figure out the other directions.
If you are facing Polaris, south will be behind you. East will be to your right and west will be to your left.
One way to find Polaris is to find the grouping of stars called the Big Dipper. Two of its stars point to Polaris.
The Big Dipper's position changes with the seasons, but it always points to Polaris. If it is a clear night, you will be able to see it.

Everyday **SCIENCE**

Geocaching

Do you enjoy scavenger hunts? Then you might like **geocaching.** It follows the same idea, but uses GPS and online clues. The goal is to find something (the "cache") that another game player has stashed in an out-of-the-way place. There are over 3 million geocaches hidden around the world.

1

First, someone hides the cache. The cache is a small box where the person places some "treasure" to be found, such as a small toy. The cache also contains a logbook.

2

The cache is hidden where it will not easily be seen, like in a hollow log, between rocks, or under a bench.

3

Next, the person who hid the cache posts clues online so players can find it. The clues include precise longitude and latitude readings.

4

The player searches for the cache using GPS. But they can only get within 30 ft (9 m) of it using GPS. Then, they have to use their senses to find it.

5

When they find the cache, the player opens the box and signs the logbook. This shows they were there.

6

The player can take the treasure out of the geocache. But if they do, they must put something else in.

Let's

EXPERIMENT!

MAKE A TREASURE MAP

Become a creative cartographer by making your own treasure map! You can make it look more realistic by staining and crumpling the paper, so it looks like it has been passed down through the ages.

You will need:

- Paper
- Cold tea or coffee
- A blow-dryer
- A pen

1 Take a piece of paper. Crumple it up into a ball. Uncrumple the paper. Lay it flat on a table or other surface.

2 Sprinkle some cold tea or coffee on the paper. The color will help it look old.

3 Dry the paper with a blow-dryer set to a low setting.

4 Use the pen to draw your map. Don't forget to add an X to mark the treasure!

A MAP FROM 1582

Maps have changed a lot over the years. This map was made in Spain in 1582. It shows South America. But really, it shows what the people who made it thought South America looked like. You might recognize some names on it, like Peru and Brazil.

Let's

EXPERIMENT!

MAKE A COMPASS

People have used compasses for hundreds of years to help them find their way. In this experiment, you will make your own.

You will need:

- A needle
- A magnet
- Adhesive putty
- A cork
- A bowl of water

1 Carefully hold a needle by the eye (the hole at the blunt end).

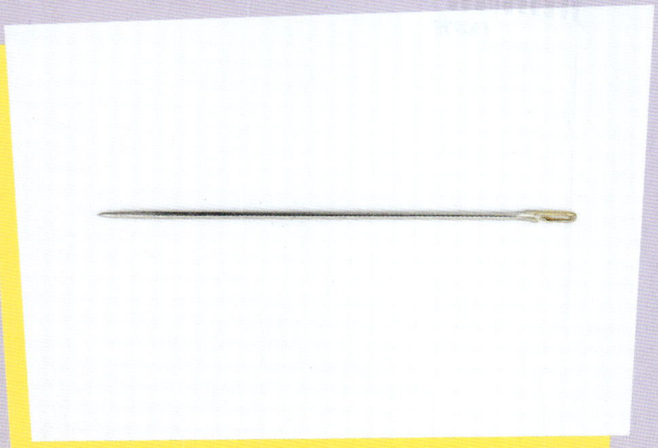

2 Rub the needle on the magnet 50 times. Make sure you lift the needle off the magnet each time.

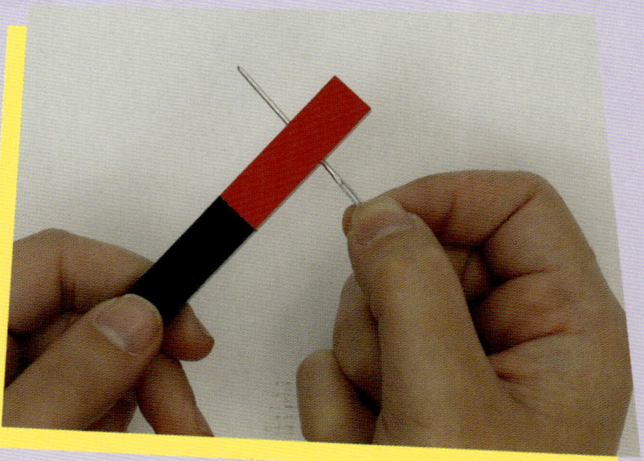

3 Put some adhesive putty on top of a cork. Then put the needle on top of the putty.

4 Get a bowl of water. Put the cork in the water. It will move until the eye of the needle is pointing north.

COMPASS CONFUSION AT THE POLES

Explorers at the North and South Poles have a tough time using compasses. Normally, a compass needle points north, but near the poles, it gets confused and may point up or down instead. Because of this, explorers use tools like GPS. They also look at the Sun and stars for direction.

Vocabulary **BUILDER**

A Hike to Remember

People use maps to navigate the great outdoors. Read the journal entry to find out how one hiker and her father ascended and descended a high mountain. Pay attention to key words that describe how the map and other tools helped them understand and plan for the terrain they would be climbing.

“After driving to the **trailhead**, Dad took out the topographic map. The mountain's elevation is 3,554 ft (1,083 m), so we knew it would be a long day.

There are two trails to the **summit**. We measured them with the map scale and ruler. The blue trail was about 3 miles (4.8 km) but the contour lines were close together at the top—a steep climb! The red trail was about 5 miles (8 km) long but looked easier.

We took the red trail up and the blue trail down. Dad handed me the compass and said I was our guide. Using the trail map and key, I kept us on track. When we reached the summit, the view was amazing! Dad used his pocket GPS to check our exact longitude and latitude, which matched the **survey marker** at the top.”